MIMI MCRAE

Travel Guide to Lewis and Harris

A Pocket Companion when exploring the Western Isles

Copyright © 2023 by Mimi McRae

All rights reserved. No part of this publication may be reproduced, stored or transmitted in any form or by any means, electronic, mechanical, photocopying, recording, scanning, or otherwise without written permission from the publisher. It is illegal to copy this book, post it to a website, or distribute it by any other means without permission.

Mimi McRae asserts the moral right to be identified as the author of this work.

Mimi McRae has no responsibility for the persistence or accuracy of URLs for external or third-party Internet Websites referred to in this publication and does not guarantee that any content on such Websites is, or will remain, accurate or appropriate.

Designations used by companies to distinguish their products are often claimed as trademarks. All brand names and product names used in this book and on its cover are trade names, service marks, trademarks and registered trademarks of their respective owners. The publishers and the book are not associated with any product or vendor mentioned in this book. None of the companies referenced within the book have endorsed the book.

Second edition

Proofreading by Stewart Wilson

This book was professionally typeset on Reedsy.
Find out more at reedsy.com

Contents

1	To Begin With:	1
2	Introduction	4
3	Stornoway	12
4	Plan Your Stay	21
5	Where to Stay	26
6	Modes of Travel	34
7	The Foodie in You	41
8	The Island Does Alcohol	47
9	Crafts, Community, and Tweed.	52
10	Hebridean Heritage Sites	61
11	Security, Health and Pets	69
12	Leisure and Recreation	73
13	Other Helpful Places	86
14	Notable Beaches of the Island	90
15	Maps	94
16	In Conclusion	103
17	Resources	106

1

To Begin With:

As you reach for this booklet, it's important to note that what you'll encounter here is not an exhaustive travel guide but a pocket companion to the Western Isles. This concise guide is intended as a starting point, a glimpse into the rich tapestry of landscapes, culture, and history these islands offer. It's a foretaste to ignite your curiosity and inspire you to explore further.

The Western Isles hold a multitude of wonders, many of which are beyond the scope of any guidebook. This booklet has highlighted some key places and experiences, but much more is waiting to be discovered. Each island has its unique character and secrets, inviting you to embark on a journey of exploration and discovery.

Please look at this booklet as your initial guidepost, pointing you toward some of the islands' most notable and captivating aspects. It's an invitation to wander, to explore beyond the beaten path, and to create your unique adventure. The true essence of the Western Isles unfolds through personal experience as you immerse yourself in the landscapes, engage with the local communities, and create connections with this enchanting part of the world.

TO BEGIN WITH:

So, as you plan your journey to the Outer Hebrides, remember that this booklet is just the beginning. A whole world of beauty, mystery, and enchantment awaits you on these islands, each with its own story and wonders to reveal. Let this guide be the first step in a journey that promises to be as rewarding as it is unforgettable.

2

Introduction

Welcome to the Western Isles

The Outer Hebrides, a remote and rugged cluster of Islands also known as the Western Isles, are a chain of islands off the west coast of mainland Scotland. They are about 24 miles northwest of the west coast of mainland Scotland, but - from port to port, it is about 54 miles, and they are known for their unique blend of natural, rugged beauty, remote location, rich history, and unique cultural heritage.

The Isle of Lewis -

The Isle of Lewis is the most significant part of the Outer Hebrides, and you would find it on a map in the northern part of these islands. It's connected to the Isle of Harris to the south, although they are often referred to as two separate islands. The Isle of Lewis is relatively flat compared to Harris, which has more mountainous terrain.

INTRODUCTION

When looking at a map, you'll typically see the town of Stornoway on the east coast of Lewis, the largest town in the Outer Hebrides. The island's coastline is irregular, with numerous inlets and bays. The landscape of Lewis is characterised by a mixture of peat bogs, a rugged coastline, and small lochs (lakes).

TRAVEL GUIDE TO LEWIS AND HARRIS

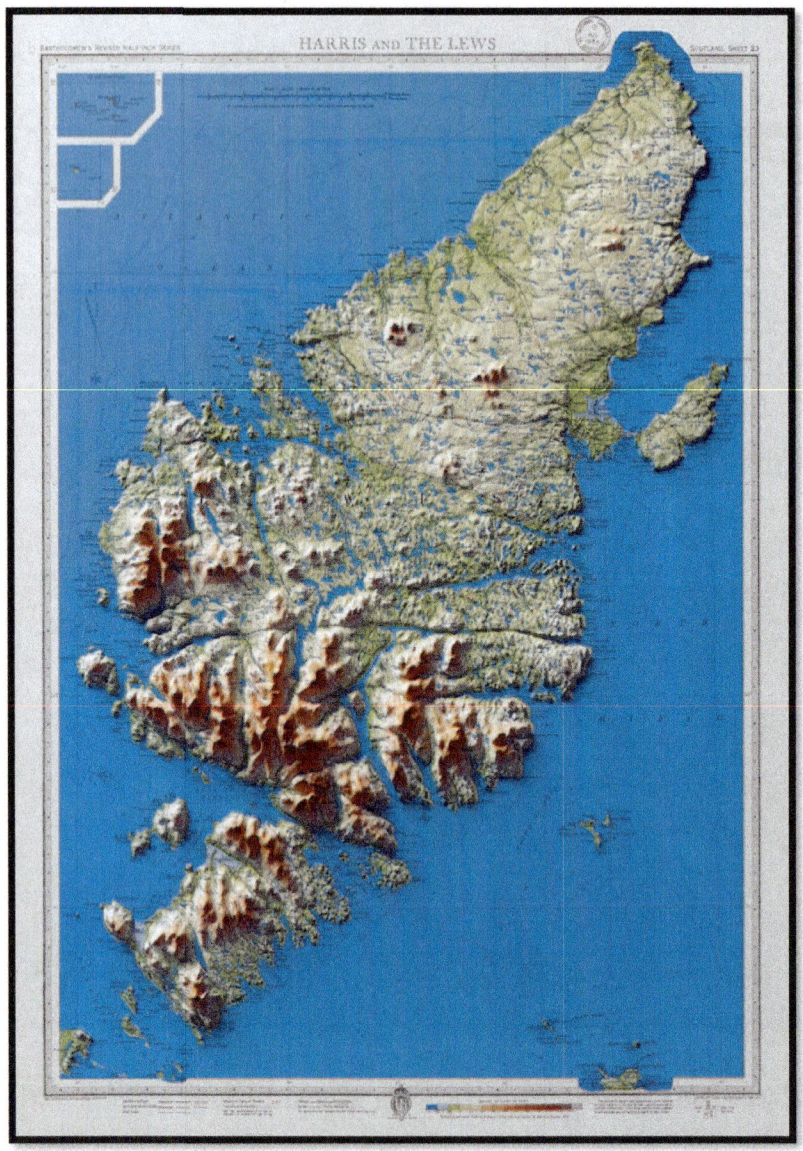

Looking at these two maps gives you an idea of the layout of the places in Lewis and the topographical layout of Lewis and Harris. The topographical map can be purchased from Printagonist on Etsy.

INTRODUCTION

Natural Beauty: The Outer Hebrides are renowned for their stunning landscapes, which include pristine sandy beaches, rolling moorlands, and rugged mountains. The beaches are particularly famous for their white sands and turquoise waters, resembling more tropical destinations.

The Isle of Lewis, the largest of the Outer Hebrides, presents a landscape teeming with natural beauty that captures the essence of Scotland's wild and untamed charm. The island is a tapestry of diverse terrains, from expansive, windswept moors that stretch to the horizon to rugged coastlines sculpted by the relentless Atlantic Ocean. This dynamic landscape offers an array of stunning vistas and photographic opportunities.

As you traverse the island, you are welcomed by the vast peatlands of the Lewis moor. This hauntingly beautiful expanse changes hues with the day's shifting light. These moors are a testament to the island's raw beauty and a crucial habitat for wildlife, including numerous bird species like the golden eagle and the elusive red grouse. The call of these birds adds a haunting soundtrack to the island's natural splendour.

The coastline of Lewis is equally breathtaking, with its dramatic cliffs that rise steeply from the sea, creating formidable natural fortresses that have withstood the test of time. The rocky shores are dotted with secluded coves and stunning beaches, such as the renowned Uig Sands, where the contrast of white sands against the dark waters offers a mesmerising sight. These coastal areas are often frequented by seals basking on the rocks, and on a lucky day, one might catch a glimpse of dolphins or whales breaching the ocean's surface.

The island has numerous lochs and still waters reflecting the ever-changing Scottish skies. The tranquillity of these lochs, surrounded by gentle hills and open skies, provides a serene backdrop for reflection and photography. The Isle of Lewis is also home to the famous Callanish Standing Stones. This prehistoric stone circle silently witnesses millennia of history. The stones, especially under the glow of the setting or rising sun, create an ethereal and almost otherworldly scene, perfect for capturing the mystical side of the island.

Seasonal changes bring their magic to Lewis. The summer months cloak the island in a blanket of green, with the Machair coming alive with a riot of wildflowers. In contrast, autumn and winter bring a more subdued but equally captivating landscape, with shorter days leading to dramatic sunsets and the chance to witness the Northern Lights dancing in the night sky.

INTRODUCTION

Every aspect of Lewis, from its ancient landscapes and rich wildlife to its serene waters and dramatic coastlines, offers a window into a world where nature reigns supreme. It's a place where photographers, nature lovers, and adventurers alike can find endless inspiration in the raw, unspoiled beauty of the Scottish Isles.

The Isle of Harris -

The Isle of Harris, the other half of the Isle of Lewis, is a place of extraordinary natural beauty, encompassing a variety of stunning landscapes and features. Some of the critical aspects of Harris's natural beauty are -

The **Spectacular Beaches**: Harris is renowned for its beautiful beaches, such as Luskentyre, Seilebost, and Horgabost, known for their expansive stretches of white sand and turquoise waters.

The **Rugged Mountains**: The North Harris hills are characterised by their dramatic, rocky terrain, including the highest peak in the Outer Hebrides, Clisham. These mountains offer challenging hikes and breathtaking views.

The **Vast Moorlands**: The island features extensive peat moorlands, a stark landscape unique to the Scottish Highlands and Islands, providing a habitat for various wildlife.

The **Machair Landscapes**: Along the west coast, the machair (a Gaelic word describing a fertile, low-lying grassy plain) is a rare habitat, blooming with wildflowers in the spring and summer and supporting a diversity of birdlife.

The **Coastal Geology**: The coastline of Harris is a mix of cliffs, natural harbours, and sea lochs sculpted by the Atlantic Ocean. The rocky shores are interspersed with hidden coves and beaches.

The **Crystal Clear Waters**: The waters surrounding Harris are remarkably clear, making it an ideal location for marine activities like snorkelling and diving, where various marine life can be observed.

The **Wildlife**: The island is home to numerous species of birds, including eagles, and its coastal areas are frequented by seals, otters, and occasionally dolphins and whales.

INTRODUCTION

The **Flora**: Harris's flora is diverse, with heather-covered hills, coastal grasslands, and unique plant species adapted to the island's varied environments.

The **Lochs and Waterways**: Freshwater lochs and streams are scattered across the island, often set in picturesque locations ideal for fishing or simply enjoying the tranquillity.

The **Photographic Landscapes**: Harris offers many opportunities for photographers, from capturing the changing moods of the beaches and mountains to the subtler details of the machair and moorland.

The natural beauty of the Isle of Harris is both dramatic and subtle, offering visitors a chance to experience a landscape that is constantly shaped and reshaped by the elements and a connection to nature that is both profound and inspiring.

3

Stornoway

When you arrive on the Isle of Lewis, the first place you will find is our main town - Stornoway, the largest town in the Outer Hebrides and the main entry point to the Isle of Lewis. It is a charming and vibrant town that offers visitors cultural, historical, and modern experiences. Here's what you can find and enjoy throughout the year in Stornoway:

Rich Cultural Heritage: As the cultural and commercial hub of the Outer Hebrides, Stornoway has a rich Gaelic heritage. Visitors can immerse themselves in this culture by attending local events, listening to traditional Gaelic music, and even trying to learn a few phrases of the Gaelic language.

Historic Sites: The town is home to noteworthy historical sites like the Lews Castle, a Victorian-era castle set in expansive grounds overlooking the harbour, built during the years of 1844 - 1851 as a country home for Sir James Matheson, who had bought the whole Island a few years prior with the profits he had made in the opium trade.

STORNOWAY

The Storehouse Café – Lews Castle.

The castle grounds are perfect for a leisurely walk, and the building now houses a museum, a cultural centre, and a reasonable-sized cafe on the ground floor: Storehouse Cafe. The Callanish Standing Stones and other sites can also be viewed up close and personal as you tour the Island.

The Storehouse Café Shop – Lews Castle

Local Arts and Crafts: Stornoway boasts a variety of local shops selling traditional Hebridean crafts, including the famous Harris Tweed, handwoven in the Outer Hebrides. Galleries also showcase local art (An Lanntair), giving visitors a taste of the island's artistic talents.

Seafood and Gastronomy: Stornoway is a port town known for its excellent seafood and the locally produced Stornoway Black Pudding. Various restaurants and cafes offer fresh, locally sourced seafood and other culinary delights. Some of the more popular ones are the Blue

Lobster, The Bridge Center Cafe, Elevens Restaurant & Bar, The Boatshed Restaurant, Harbour Kitchen, Buth An Rubdh, Artizan, Harris and Lewis Smokehouse, Stornoway Balti House, Big Bite, Golden Ocean, Istanbul Indian Restaurant, The Fank, Bangla Spice, The Thai, The New Lewis Bar and the No9 Coffee Shop & Cocktail Bar.

Harbor and Marina: The bustling harbour and marina are central to life in Stornoway. It's enjoyable to watch the comings and goings of fishing boats and yachts or to take a leisurely stroll along the quay, with or without some fish and chips that can be found at Cameron's Chip shop, The Big Bite and the Church Street Chippy. Many cruise ships come to visit these islands, with work currently in progress for a large berth closer to Stornoway. The **Inner Harbour Marina** can hold boats up to 24 m long and 3 m draft in all weather conditions and is right next to the town centre. Amenities available to marina users are Toilets/showers, Shore power, Fuel berth, Gas supplies, Petrol available, Repair facilities, Chandlery, and Wi-Fi. **Newton Marina** opened in May 2021 with a 75-berth facility for long-term stays, can hold vessels of 15 m with a draft of 2.5 m, and shore power is available.

Festivals and Events: Stornoway hosts several festivals and events throughout the year, including the Hebridean Celtic Festival, which attracts international artists and visitors. These events are a great way to experience the local culture and community spirit. The most well-known of these festivals is the HebCelt.

The Outer Hebrides resonate with the soul-stirring tunes of traditional music. Fiddles, bagpipes, and accordions echo through village halls and pubs, carrying the islands' spirit. Local musicians often gather for impromptu sessions, creating an atmosphere where the boundary between performer and audience blurs, and everyone becomes part of the musical experience. Traditional music plays a vital role in island life. There are numerous music festivals throughout the year, showcasing both local talent and artists from other fields. These festivals are a great way to experience the local culture and community spirit.

The HebCelt - Hebridean Celtic Festival (Scottish Gaelic: Fèis Cheilteach Innse Gall) is the most popular and well-known of the music festivals and began around 1996. It is held annually in Stornoway (in mid-July) and has won numerous awards and commendations. It is a vibrant celebration of local music and culture showcasing a fusion of traditional and Celtic music with a capacity of 16,000. The festival attracts performers from across the globe, creating an unforgettable experience for visitors. Performers to date include Runrig, Van Morrison, Deacon Blue, The Proclaimers, Blazing Fiddles, Shooglenifty, Capercaillie, Seth Lakeman, Red Hot Chilli Pipers, Saw Doctors, The Water Boys, The Fratellis, Julie Fowlis, The Levellers, Peatbog Fairies, and KT Tunstall. The festival not only celebrates the rich musical heritage of the islands but also serves as a bridge between the past and the present.

With tickets ranging in price from £9 for an infant to an adult weekend pass of £155, you shouldn't be surprised to hear that early bird tickets sell out quickly. Go to www.Hebceltfest.com for more information on past and upcoming events.

Natural Surroundings: Though it's a town, Stornoway is surrounded by the natural beauty characteristic of the Hebrides. Nearby are beaches, coastal walks, and nature reserves, offering easy access to the serene landscapes of the island. You will need a car to reach most of these beaches and walks as they begin about 6 miles outside of the centre of Stornoway: Traigh Ghearadha, Bosta Beach, Dalmore Beach, Traigh Mhor, Uig Sands, Coll Beach, Traigh Lar Beach, Mangersta Beach and Scarista Beach to name a few.

Shopping and Amenities: The main town, Stornoway is well-equipped with shops, supermarkets (Tesco and Co-Op), and other amenities, making it a convenient base for visitors exploring the island. Pets are welcome on the ferry (ask for a pet ticket to take your pet onboard) and on the Island. The Veterinary practice - Old Mill Vets on Sandwick Road, Stornoway, can handle all your pet needs while you visit the Island.

Accommodations: There are various accommodation options, from hotels and guest houses to Bed & Breakfast, Air BnBs and self-catering cottages, catering to different preferences and budgets. Some Larger hotels in Stornoway are The Royal Hotel, The Cabarfeidh, The Caladh Inn, The County Hotel, The Crown, and the Lews Castle.

Community Hub: The town is the social and administrative heart of the island, with a friendly community atmosphere. Visitors often find a warm welcome and an opportunity to interact with residents. Stornoway, with its blend of history, culture, and modern conveniences, set against the backdrop of the stunning Hebridean landscape, offers a unique and enriching experience for visitors to the Isle of Lewis.

Weather: The island experiences distinct seasonal runs: winter spans from December to February, spring from March to May, summer from June to August, and autumn from September to November. However, the weather on the island is a different story altogether. Regardless of the season, you might encounter various weather conditions, from gentle to strong winds, light to heavy rain, and skies ranging from clear to overcast. Typically, the winter gales roar through in February, while May tends to be quite wet. Snow is a rare guest here, seldom settling for long. When it does stick around, it typically lasts a few days to a week, disappearing until the following year. This brief tenure of snow is attributed to the tempering effects of the Gulf Stream on the local climate. Summer days usually hover around 15°C (59°F), but with prolonged sunny spells, temperatures can soar up to 23°C (73°F). In contrast, autumn brings cooler temperatures, generally between 10°C and 6°C (50°F to 42°F), while winter sees temperatures ranging from a mild 7°C down to a cooler 2°C (44°F to 35°F).

This island's beauty shines through regardless of the weather, offering abundant experiences. From the picturesque landscapes perfect for photography enthusiasts to a rich array of local foods waiting to be savoured, there's always something to capture your senses. Immerse yourself in the melodious local music and the unique Gaelic language, or revel in the vibrant atmosphere of summer music festivals. The island's trails and pristine beaches beckon for the adventurous, while Sea-Trek offers a day trip to the Isle of St Kilda. Don't miss the chance to taste the region's new whiskeys and the distinctive Harris Gin. As the day draws to a close, imagine warming yourself with a crackling open log fire indoors or under the stars, where toasting marshmallows could be the perfect end to your day.

STORNOWAY

WI-FI For Mobile Signal

The Isle of Lewis, while rich in natural beauty and cultural heritage, faces the challenge of limited cellular and Wi-Fi connectivity in many areas. Despite ongoing efforts to improve digital infrastructure, several parts of the island still experience inconsistent or non-existent cellular reception and Wi-Fi access. This digital divide is particularly evident in more remote and rural locations, where the rugged terrain and the dispersed nature of communities pose significant obstacles to establishing comprehensive network coverage. The lack of reliable internet and mobile phone services affects residents' daily lives, hindering communication and access to online resources and impacting local businesses and tourism. Efforts by both governmental and private entities continue to focus on enhancing digital connectivity across the island, recognising its importance for economic development, education, healthcare, and social inclusion. However, as of now, the reality for many living in or visiting certain parts of the Isle of Lewis is a degree of digital isolation, emblematic of the challenges that remote and rural communities face in today's increasingly connected world.

4

Plan Your Stay

So you have decided to visit the Western Isles. Wonderful!

Next question - What to pack?

When planning your trip to the Western Isles, your packing list will largely depend on the time of year you visit and the duration of your stay. Regardless of these factors, a key piece of advice is to reserve some space in your suitcase for purchases you'll inevitably make on the island. Souvenirs and gifts are hard to resist, and as I once read, "Nothing haunts you more than that 'thing' you did not buy." This may not literally haunt you, but it can certainly leave you with a tinge of regret.

Based on my 24 years (and counting) of living here, I recommend packing in layers. Opt for a light but rain-proof coat or jacket and clothes you can mix and match, suitable for dining out and attending a Ceilidh (pronounced Kay-lee, a Scottish dance or party). Don't forget a warm hat – an essential item in this climate.

Arriving by air offers several routes: flights might connect through London Heathrow (Terminal 5), Amsterdam, Glasgow, Inverness, Edinburgh, or even Dublin. The choice depends on your airline and booking preferences. Remember, there is only one airport on the Isle of Lewis, with flight prices varying based on the provider and travel season.

If you asked me the best time to visit the Western Isles, I'd suggest mid-April to late June. This period offers the most favourable weather but also comes with higher costs for hotels and flights, and bookings can be challenging to secure at short notice. I would advise against visiting in February unless you're accustomed to harsh weather. This is the month of intense storms, with winds reaching up to 115 mph, particularly in Uist's more exposed lower islands. Travel during this time, whether by ferry or flight, can be pretty tumultuous, often leading to seasickness or flight disruptions.

PLAN YOUR STAY

For those arriving by car, you have two main ferry entry points: Stornoway (Lewis) and Tarbert (Harris). The Stornoway ferry, departing from Ullapool, takes about 2 hours and 30 minutes, while the Tarbert ferry from Uig on the Isle of Skye takes roughly 1 hour and 45 minutes. Both routes are operated by Caledonian MacBrayne, commonly known as 'CalMac Ferries.' You can find timetables and prices on their website –www.calmac.co.uk, and it is advisable to book a few weeks in advance, especially for car spaces on the ferry, as they start filling up as the summer months approach.

Please see the following two pictures to give you an idea of the cost of cars and passengers on the ferry to Stornoway in Lewis (from Ullapool) and Tarbert in Harris (from Uig in the Isle of Skye). Prices can change, so please check with Calmac's website.

FARES

Stornoway - Ullapool		Single	Return
Driver/passenger		£10.25	£20.50
Child 5-15 (Infant under 5 free, must have a valid ticket)		£5.15	£10.30
Car or 4x4 (excludes driver)		£55.75	£111.50
Motorhome (excludes driver)	Up to 6m	£55.75	£111.50
	Up to 8m	£139.40	£278.80
	Up to 10m	£167.25	£334.50
Caravan, boat/baggage trailer	Up to 2.5m	£27.90	£55.80
	Up to 6m	£55.75	£110.50
	Up to 8m	£83.65	£167.30
Motorcycle		£27.90	£55.80
Pedal cycles (restricted numbers)		Free	Free
Groups of 6 or more pedal cycles must inform the relevant port office in advance of travel. It should be noted that as we may not be able to offer the first sailing of choice, therefore groups may not always be able to travel together			
Light goods vehicles exceeding 6 metres in length or 3.5 tonnes in weight, or 3 metres in height, or 2.3 metres in width are charged at commercial vehicle rate			

FARES

Uig - Tarbert		Single	Return
Driver/passenger		£6.85	£13.70
Child 5-15 (Infant under 5 free, must have a valid ticket)		£3.45	£6.90
Car or 4x4 (excludes driver)		£33.85	£67.70
Motorhome (excludes driver)	Up to 6m	£33.85	£67.70
	Up to 8m	£84.65	£169.30
	Up to 10m	£101.55	£203.10
Caravan, boat/baggage trailer	Up to 2.5m	£16.95	£33.90
	Up to 6m	£33.85	£67.70
	Up to 8m	£50.80	£101.60
Motorcycle		£16.95	£33.90
Pedal cycles (restricted numbers)		Free	Free
Groups of 6 or more pedal cycles must inform the relevant port office in advance of travel. It should be noted that as we may not be able to offer the first sailing of choice, therefore groups may not always be able to travel together			
Light goods vehicles exceeding 6 metres in length or 3.5 tonnes in weight, or 3 metres in height, or 2.3 metres in width are charged at commercial vehicle rate			

Embarking on the ferry to the Isle of Lewis, you can dine against the backdrop of Scotland's breathtaking seascapes. Breakfast on this journey is a serene affair; as the early morning sun casts golden hues over the water, passengers enjoy traditional Scottish fare - perhaps porridge sweetened with local honey or a hearty, full Scottish breakfast. The rhythmic motion of the ferry complements the peaceful start to the day. As noon approaches, the lunch served is a delightful interlude featuring fresh, locally sourced seafood, a nod to the island's rich maritime heritage. The dining area, with panoramic views of the churning sea and distant shores, provides a mesmerising setting. As evening falls, dinner on the ferry becomes a reflective experience. The menu often features heart-warming classics, with ingredients hailing from the bountiful Scottish Highlands and islands. Dining as the ferry glides through the Hebrides, with the sunset painting the sky in brilliant shades, the day's meals transcend mere sustenance, becoming integral to the soulful journey to Lewis.

5

Where to Stay

WHERE TO STAY

For those looking to indulge in a luxurious experience, the castle, complete with a museum, offers an ideal stay. Constructed from 1844 - 1851 by Sir James Matheson following his purchase of the island a few years previously, this historic castle now houses a beautiful array of rooms and apartments, including one that is pet-friendly. In addition to its accommodation, the castle features The

Storehouse Cafe, a spacious and inviting coffee shop open to both castle residents and the public. This makes it a perfect spot to relax and enjoy hot food and drinks after visiting the museum, where the original Lewis Chessmen are displayed, or taking a leisurely walk around the castle grounds. The cafe is conveniently open daily from 10 am to 4 pm.

Five larger hotels are in Stornoway and two in Tarbert (Harris). There are four hotels in the centre of Stornoway:

- **The Royal Hotel** - Cromwell Street, Stornoway, HS1 2DG. Tel: 01851 702109.
- **The Caladh Inn** - 11 James St, Stornoway, HS1 2QN. Tel: 01851 702740.
- **The County Hotel** - 12-14 Francis St, Stornoway, HS1 2XB. Tel: 01851 703250.
- **The Crown** - Stornoway, HS1 2BD. Tel: 01851 703734.

WHERE TO STAY

The Lews Castle, Museum, Cafe, and Suites is situated inside the Grounds and gardens of the Stornoway trust.

- **Lews Castle** - Stornoway. Tel: 01625 416 430.

The Caberfeidh (pronounced 'Caber-fey') is on the outer edge of Stornoway.

- **The Caberfeidh** - Manor Park, Perceval Rd South, Stornoway, HS1 2EU. Tel: 01851 702604.

Prices for rooms per night at these hotels typically range from £122 to £200.

Each hotel has its restaurant and bar, which are also open to the public. Bed & breakfast facilities are dotted all over the Island, in every village, along with some charming 'Air bnb' homes. There is also a Hostel on Kenneth Street in Stornoway:

- **Heb Hostel** - 25 Kenneth St, Stornoway, HS1 2DR. Tel: 01851 709889.

There are two hotels in Tarbert. The biggest one is the Harris Hotel, found on the left just before the turn into Tarbert. The other hotel, Hotel Hebrides, is located nearer the Tarbert ferry terminal.

- **Harris Hotel** - Scott Rd, Tarbert, Isle of Harris, HS3 3DL. Tel: 01859 502154.

- **Hotel Hebrides** - Pier Rd, Tarbert, Isle of Harris, HS3 3DG. Tel: 01859 502364.

During the tourist season, which typically runs from the end of May to the end of September, various outdoor accommodations are available, including wild camping, camping, caravanning, and tenting. Outside Stornoway, in Laxdale, and across Harris, there are designated areas for camping, tents, and parking mobile homes or caravans. Those interested in wild camping should note that much of the land in Lewis's villages is divided into 'Crofts,' privately owned by families or individuals. Harris offers more opportunities for wild camping thanks to its more immense expanse of 'common grazing' land. However, it's essential to remember that some areas may still be privately owned. Additionally, when wild camping, be prepared for encounters with local wildlife, including wandering sheep and cows. Sometimes, if you're in the right place at the right time, you might even find curious deer observing your activities.

WHERE TO STAY

When it comes to beaches, we are truly blessed here. Beaches? Yes, we have them in abundance – from serene stretches of sand to lively shores where the sea is just a stone's throw away, depending on the direction of the wind.

Imagine waking up to the scent of sea salt and seaweed, a quintessential island morning. For the adventurous, a morning dip in the sea might be the perfect start to the day. If that's a bit too daring, perhaps a leisurely barefoot walk along the beach, sipping your morning beverage as the wind tousles your hair and plays with your clothes, would be more to your liking.

So, if you're considering bringing a tent, caravan, or mobile home – and even your family pet – I say go for it. It's an opportunity for a photogenic and wholesome adventure. As for the beaches in Lewis and Harris, I will detail some notable ones later in this booklet, but feel free to skip ahead and take a peek if you can't wait.

Camping sites for mobile homes can be found in both Lewis and Harris.

- **Callanish Camping Pods** - Pier Road, Callanish, Stornoway, Isle of Lewis HS2 9DY. Tel: 07809330971.
- **Laxdale Holiday Park** - 6 Laxdale Ln, Laxdale, Isle of Lewis HS2 0DR. Tel: 01581 706966.
- **Horgabost** campsite - Horgabost Township, Isle of Harris HS3 3HR. Tel: 1859 550386.
- **Barra Sands** Campsite - 12, Western Isles, Eoligarry, Isle of Barra HS9 5YD. Tel: 07786422954.
- **Seilebost School** Campsite - (West Harris Trust) Isle of Harris HS3 3HP. Tel: 01859 503900.
- **Huisinis** Campsite - Huisinis Gateway, Isle of Harris HS3 3AY. Tel: 01859 502222.
- **Talla na Marra** Caravan and Motorhome Campsite - Talla na Mara Horgabost, Isle of Harris HS3 3AE. Tel: 01859 503901.

- Park Niseabost (7 pitches by Talla na Marra) - A859, Isle of Harris HS3 3AE. Tel: 01859 503901.
- **Eilean Fraoich** Camp Site - N. Shawbost, Isle of Lewis, HS2 9BQ. Tel: 01851 710504 - "it is about £20 per night for a touring van".
- **Minch View** Campsite - 10 Drinishader, Isle of Harris, HS3 3DX. Tel: 01859 511207 - "Definitely a 'no frills' campsite, but everything you need is there".

I have tried to supply the correct details here, but please keep in mind that phone numbers can change over time, and to ensure you get to the right place you want, double-check the contact details on the Web.

6

Modes of Travel

Delving deeper into the various transportation options available for reaching the Western Isles, this chapter aims to provide detailed insights, helping you make an informed decision about your travel to this region known for its stunning landscapes and rich culture.

Stornoway has just one airport with flights operated by Logan Air. Some of the routes flown are:

- Glasgow - Stornoway: 1 hour flight time.
- Glasgow to Barra: 1 hour flight time (lands on the beach).
- Glasgow to Benbecula: I hour flight time.
- Edinburgh to Stornoway: 1 hour flight time.
- Inverness to Stornoway: flight time 30 mins.
- Inverness to Benbecula via Stornoway: 1 hour flight time.
- Stornoway to Benbecula: flight time 30 mins.
- Manchester to Stornoway: 2 hours 55 min flight time.

MODES OF TRAVEL

Flights arrive (through connection flights into Inverness) from places further afield such as Birmingham, Amsterdam, and London Heathrow Terminal 5. Flight prices vary greatly and depend on who you book with, whether it was booked directly with your carrier, the time of year, and who/what you are travelling with. From personal experience, the cheapest time to book a flight is six weeks before you travel and to book directly with your carrier.

The ferry service to the Island arrives at three different locations. Two are in Harris, and one is in Stornoway.

- **Stornoway Ferry Terminal** - From Ullapool. - 2 hours 30 mins.
- **Harris Ferry Terminal** - From Uig (Skye). - 1 hour 40 mins.
- **Uig Ferry Terminal (Skye)** - Lochmaddy (North Uist). - 1 hour 45 minutes.
- **Berneray Ferry Terminal** - Leverburgh (Harris). - 1 hour.

All further information, times, and prices for these journeys can be found on the Calmac.co.uk website. Or if you can't get to the internet, you can call them at 0800 066 5000, +44 1475 650397 (for international customers), or email enquiries@calmac.co.uk. They also have Twitter for the latest service updates: @CalMac_Updates where they aim to answer any questions you send them between 8 am-8 pm, seven days a week.

Once you arrive, options for reaching the town centre include - limited bus service, private car hire, and taxis directly from the arrival lounge. The bus journey to Stornoway is brief, taking about 5 - 7 minutes, with fares currently around £12 as the local council runs them and buses may not supply guaranteed 'link-up' services with flights. Alternatively, a pre-booked taxi could be cost-effective, especially if you're not picking up a hire car or being met by friends or family. This is particularly economical if carpooling, as the cost is shared among passengers. Numerous taxi services supply Stornoway and surrounding villages. There are too many to list here, but below are a few names and numbers if you need something quickly. Please remember that not all taxis are available on a Sunday, so it is better to book in advance if you know you will need one.

- Alpha Taxis - 07553 374210.
- A1 Taxis - 07818 216970.
- Associated - 01581 702300.
- ATS Taxis - 01581 703028.
- Barbara - 07884 197455.
- Calum - 07799 128537.
- D M's Taxi - 07399 008046.
- MM Taxis - 01581 700013.
- 24:7 - 01581 702424.
- STS - 01851 704444.
- So that you know, all of these numbers should be dialled from within the UK.

For those preferring to rent a car, Hebrides Car Hire, located at the airport, is a convenient option. They also have outlets at the Stornoway ferry terminal and near the Harris Hotel in Tarbert, offering both cars and vans, with one-way hires available through their website. A helpful tip for travellers from the USA: in the UK, fuel pump handles are colour-coded differently – green for petrol (gasoline) and black for diesel. Remember, in the UK, you fill up your car before paying at the station, where you can also grab snacks.

- **Hebrides Car Hire** - Ferry Terminal, Shell Street, Stornoway, HS1

2AE. Tel: 01851 706500.

Stornoway has three petrol stations: The Spar Filling Station, Engebrets Ltd (both open for a few hours on Sundays), and Campbells (Gulf). All these stations have well-stocked shops and offer small hot takeaway foods.

- **The Spar Shop & Manor Filling Station** - 64-68 Bayhead, Stornoway HS1 2DZ. Tel: 01851 701924. Hours are 7am - 11pm. Sunday: 12 - 6pm.
- **Engebrets Ltd** - Sandwick Road Filling Station, Sandwick Rd, Stornoway HS1 2SL. Tel: 01851 702303. Hours are 6am - 11pm. Sunday: 10am - 4pm.
- **Campbells (Gulf)** - Cannery Rd, Stornoway HS1 2SF. Tel: 01851 702127. Hours are 7am - 11pm. Closed on Sunday.

Consider cycle hire for a more active and intimate experience with the elements. Two establishments in Stornoway, Bike Hebrides and BeSpoke Bicycles (Hebrides) Ltd, offer bike rentals. BeSpoke, in addition to rentals, provides bicycle repair services (Bronze, Silver, Gold, Suspension Fork and Emergency services) and has a café - The Hub, making it a great pit stop for cyclists needing repairs, services, or just a break.

- **BeSpoke Bicycles - The Hub**, Glen House, Willowglen Road, Stornoway, Isle of Lewis, HS1 2EP. Tel: 1851 288264 / 0787 657 0932 / bespokebicyclerepairs@gmail.com
- **Bike Hebrides** - 6 Sand St, Stornoway HS1 2UE. Tel: 07775 943355.

The Hub, situated above BeSpoke, is right on the edge of the castle grounds, perfect for dog walkers and trekkers alike. Indulge in delectable coffees, including a monthly 'Speciality Roast' from the Inverness Coffee Roasting Company and a vast array of loose-leaf teas from the Wee Tea Company. Those beverages perfectly complement their delicious, in-house, hand-made scones, cakes, pastries, and cheesecakes. At the HUB Café, you'll find a growing menu that caters to all tastes, featuring hot breakfasts for both vegetarians and meat lovers, a wide range of hot filled rolls for both preferences and delightful soups served with a hearty slice of bread from the local Blackhouse Bakery. Additionally, the cafe has introduced a tempting variety of filled, toasted bagels. They welcome all guests, including four-legged friends, who are accommodated downstairs in their cosy lounge area. So, step in and unwind with a cuppa in the comfortable setting of Glen House. For those on a tight schedule, there's no need to miss out – swing by for a quick takeaway. Rest assured, their commitment to sustainability is reflected in their fully recyclable cups, so you can enjoy your treat while contributing positively to the environment.

Buses travel most of the Island at different times of the day. The more used routes are from Stornoway to Point, Lochs, West-side, and Ness. There are also all the small villages along those routes. Buses are operated by three or four companies, with the council having its own small fleet to service Stornoway and the immediate area. Buses from Stornoway to Harris run every 2 - 3 hours - W10 - Stornoway - Tarbert (the journey takes about an hour) and W10A Tarbert - Leverburgh and Rodel every 1 -3 hours and takes about 45 minutes. More details can be found at the Bus Station in Stornoway.

- **Stornoway Bus Station** - Stornoway HS1 2BS. Tel: 01851 704327.

Finally, for those interested in walking or hiking, Lewis offers a unique opportunity. The island is approximately 50 miles long (as the crow flies) and varies in width from 10 to 12 miles from water to water. Almost every settlement is within one and a half miles of the sea. A main road runs from Stornoway, around the Clisham (which peaks about 800 m high), to Tarbert and beyond. According to Google, the walk from Stornoway to Tarbert is roughly 12 hours and 50 minutes, though this could vary with the weather.

This guide to transportation options in the Western Isles should help you plan your journey effectively, ensuring a smooth and enjoyable start to your adventure in this breathtaking region.

7

The Foodie in You

For the Foodie in you

When planning a stay on the island, particularly over a weekend, it's crucial to remember that island shops are closed on Sundays. This means most people complete their grocery shopping on Fridays or Saturdays.

The smaller shops typically close around 5:30 pm to 6 pm, while the larger ones shut their doors between 10 pm and midnight. Please remember that alcohol sales end at 10 pm across all stores, in line with Scottish regulations, so make any purchases in good time to enjoy your evening drink.

Stornoway's town centre is a haven for coffee and tea lovers, with many cafes to choose from. Noteworthy ones include Kopi Java on Cromwell Street, the Woodland Centre near the castle, and the café inside the Castle. Many shops also offer takeaway cups for those on the go.

If you're in the mood for a takeaway or 'chippy,' Stornoway offers a variety of options. Choose from Indian meals, two Chinese outlets, a Thai restaurant (where you can bring your wine), and two popular chip shops: Cameron's Chip Shop and the Church Street Chippy. In Scotland, 'chips' refer to deep-fried potato sticks, often served with salt, vinegar, and a drink like Irn Bru.

Missed breakfast in your eagerness to explore? No worries. There are several great spots for a bite. Besides the cafes mentioned earlier, there's the pet-friendly 'The Blue Lobster' near the central town's small car park, the HS1 eatery affiliated with the Royal Hotel, and 'The Boatshed Restaurant'. The Caladh Inn's Eleven Restaurant offers a carvery, and for quick bites, Tesco and Co-Op are good options. If you have kids, Adventure Island, located behind Tesco, lets them play while you relax with nice food and drink.

- **Adventure Island** - 10 Inaclete Rd, Stornoway, HS1 2RB. Tel: 01581 709865.

THE FOODIE IN YOU

Adventure Island - Stornoway

There are restaurants across the island for evening dining, from those within the four major hotels in Stornoway to more remote locations like the Uig Sands Restaurant. This restaurant offers excellent food and stunning views, perfect for a memorable dining experience. While there might be a chance of rain, it often clears up, leaving a fantastic view, and for those not driving, a post-meal 'snifter' is a delightful option.

- **Uig Sands Restaurant** - Timsgearraidh, Isle of Lewis HS2 9ET. Tel: 01851 672334.

Wanderlog.com suggests you try these 15 places:

1. **Harbour Kitchen** - 5 Cromwell St, Stornoway HS1 2DB.
2. **Uig Sands Restaurant** - Timsgearraidh, Isle of Lewis HS2 9ET.
3. **Boatshed Restaurant** - inside the Royal Hotel, Stornoway
4. **Pierhouse Cafe and Restaurant** - Pier Rd, Tarbert, Isle of Harris

HS3 3DG.
5. **North Harbour Bistro** - North Harbour, Isle of Scalpay HS4 3XU.
6. **Flavour Restaurant** - Unit 1, lomairt an obain, Tarbert, Isle of Harris HS3 3DS.
7. **Lorna's Larder** - marina, Tarbert HS3 3DJ.
8. **Crown Hotel** - Stornoway HS1 2BD.
9. **Cross Inn** - Cross, Isle of Lewis HS2 0SN.
10. **Butty Bus** - Leverburgh Harbour, Harris, United Kingdom
11. **Church Street Chippy** - Church Street, Stornoway.
12. **Elevens Restaurant and Bar** - 11 James St, Stornoway HS1 2QN.
13. **Thai** - 27 Church St, Stornoway HS1 2JD.
14. **HS1 Cafe Bar** - Cromwell St, Stornoway HS1 2DG
15. **Pronto Pizza** - 7 Bank Street, Eilean Siar, Stornoway HS1 2XG.

Every dining experience, regardless of the location, should be a sensory journey that delights and captivates. It's not just about the food on the plate; it's about the symphony of flavours that dance on your palate, the aromatic scents that tantalise your senses, and the ambience surrounding you, creating a unique backdrop for every bite. Each meal should be more than just sustenance; it should be a memorable experience, a moment in time where the setting, smells, and tastes converge to leave a lasting impression, whether it's a simple home-cooked dish or a gourmet meal in a fancy restaurant, the joy of eating lies in savouring every aspect of the meal - the flavours, the aromas, and the atmosphere.

For those who are patient and quiet enough, you might even glimpse the mythical rural Haggis when you are out and about. Charles MacLeod, a local butcher known as 'Charlie Barley', sells delicious Haggis and has won awards for his world-famous black pudding. A small portion of black pudding, perfect for a fried breakfast any day of the week, is reasonably priced (current price as of 2023).

Charles MacLeod – Butcher shop with world famous Black Pudding.

8

The Island Does Alcohol

This nicely takes me to my next point - Island whiskey and Gin. There are other whiskeys and gins that can be purchased on the island but the excitement for the island in this venue is that it has finally made its own whiskey and gin.

Established in 2015, the distillery in Tarbert is where the renowned Gin is crafted, hand-bottled, and packaged. This distinctive Gin is a blend of sugar kelp and seven meticulously selected botanicals: juniper, coriander seeds, cubebs, cassia bark, angelica root, bitter orange peel, and licorice root. The key ingredient, sugar kelp, is sourced and dried by the Hebridean Seaweed Company located just outside of Stornoway.

Not only does the distillery produce this unique Gin, but it also features a shop where visitors can purchase a range of items. These include elegantly designed glasses that echo the aesthetic of their glass gin bottles, alongside an array of soaps, dry teas, and gin refills for the bottles. The idea here is to extend the life and enjoyment of these beautifully crafted bottles through refills, rather than relegating them to recycling. Additionally, the distillery offers tours during the summer, providing an insightful peek into their gin-making process. These tours are popular and require pre-booking, which can easily be done through their website at www.harrisdistillery.com.

The Harris Distillery has recently added a historic milestone to its repertoire with the launch of its whiskey in September 2023, named the Hearach single malt, a reference to the island's heritage. This whiskey is a revival of the distilling traditions lost during the Pabbay clearances of the 1940s and is celebrated for its elegance, complexity, and character. Crafted entirely by local residents, every drop of this unique spirit is a testament to the island's distinct flavours and traditions. The distillery itself embraces a philosophy of patience and quality, stating, "Ours is a slow whiskey, and we look forward to sharing it at a different pace." This addition is sure to be a must-try for whiskey enthusiasts.

Further enriching the local whiskey scene is a small distillery located in the remote area of Uig, in Carnish on Lewis. They offer tours for those interested in discovering the intricacies of their whiskey, known as Abhainn Dearg, providing an intimate glimpse into the craft of whiskey-making.

In the heart of Stornoway, the Island Spirit Whiskey Shop serves as a treasure trove for whiskey connoisseurs. The shop caters to refined tastes with an extensive selection of whiskeys available in various sizes, from full-sized bottles to miniature ones perfect for travel. Alongside the renowned Harris Gin, available as a single bottle or in a boxed set, the shop also offers exquisite dram glasses. I purchased these glasses for my husband last year and a distinguished 16-year-old Balvenie bottle as a special gift for our 30th anniversary.

Island Spirit Whiskey Shop - 38 Cromwell St, Stornoway HS1 2DD. Tel: 07555697540.

The Harris Distillery - Tarbert, Isle of Harris, HS3 3DJ. Tel: 01859 502212. www.harrisdistillery.com

Abhainn Dearg Distillery - Carnish Isle of Lewis Outer Hebrides Scotland HS2 9EX. Tel: 07399014193.

9

Crafts, Community, and Tweed.

So, Gin and Whiskey are specialised crafts. There are other crafts on the island, too. The most well-known one worldwide is Harris Tweed. There is so much made with Harris tweed, but this island is where it calls home. On some early nights, when it's quiet and you are standing outside, you can hear the distinct sound of the looms at work: 'clackity CLACK, clackity CLACK.' Once you hear the distinct sound, it is not a sound that you would easily forget.

Many of the small house crafters use Harris Tweed in their work, and the results can be found being sold in the Spring, Summer, Autumn, and Christmas craft fairs, which are held in the town Hall in Stornoway.

Community Shops

Communities are now running their own 'community shops,' and visitors are always welcome. There are quite a few, so I will list what I can of them here, and you can pop them into your plans if you are heading through any of those areas.

Lewis Areas for local small community shops:

Stornoway: Cearns (pronounced 'Key-Yarns') Community shop.

Ness: Cross Stores (Swainbost Village)
- Common Eachdrarich (pronounced 'E - ach [ch as in 'loch] - De-rry'

A shop with 'touristy' items/coffee shop / Gallery/museum
● Petrol Pumps - petrol services and a small food shop.

Borve:
● Clan McQuarrie - a welcome meeting place for all the community

Carloway: (Carloway Village)
● A village shop which welcomes tourists

Point: (Knock Village)
● Buth an Rubha (pronounced - boo an roo-ah)
● Cafe Roo can be found in the same building as Buth an Rubha.

Uig:
● Uig community shop - a very well-stocked little shop.

Tolsta:
● A nice little shop servicing the community and all who visit.

Harris Areas for local small community shops:

Leverburgh:
● Leverburgh Hub - Cafe and Laundry facility
● Butty Bus (Leverburgh Ferry Terminal) - hot drinks and hot food to take away

Northton (and beyond):
● Hebrides People (formerly Seallam) - Tracing genealogy for anyone wanting to find their roots in the Islands, and they have an unrivalled collection of Island books on sale to the public.

CRAFTS, COMMUNITY, AND TWEED.

● Talla A Mara is a community hub/gift shop/restaurant/art gallery/-Campervan hook-up. This palace can be found on the road from Tarbert to Leverburgh.

When driving, cycling, or walking the roads in Harris, it would be remiss of me not to mention that some of the roads are 'single track with passing places.' So take care and know what might be coming over that next ridge. You will find some of these types of roads in Lewis, but they would be more profound in the small villages away from the main roads.

For the 'Crafter' in you - (Island soaps, tweed, wool, knittings.)

Stornoway, the heart of the Western Isles, offers a variety of unique shopping experiences that cater to those looking for local crafts and hidden treasures. The town hosts a 'local craft fair' three or four times yearly in the Town Hall. This event is a treasure trove of unique items, including artwork, delectable fudge, perfumes, handmade jewellery, island-made hats and gloves, works of tweed, and more. The items, often seasonal and always unique, are perfect for those seeking something distinctive.

In addition to the craft fair, Stornoway has four charity shops: British Red Cross, Bethesda, Blythswood, and the Gambia Partnership. Each offers a range of hidden gems, especially appealing to crafting enthusiasts, at affordable prices. Another notable stop is 'Tweedtastic' on Stornoway's main street, near the Shawbost Mill Tweed Shop.

Breasclete, a small village near Callanish, boasts a craft shop specialising in handmade soaps with various unique scents, from 'smokey peat' to 'lemon'. This shop offers hard and liquid soaps, creams, balms, wedding favours, accessories, and candles, all made using high-quality ingredients from the Isle of Lewis. Their full range of products is displayed on their website.

For knitting and wool enthusiasts, there is a shop in Stornoway: Wool for Ewe, though it may soon relocate to Balallan, a village en route to Harris. Balallan is the third village you'll encounter when travelling from Stornoway towards Harris, after Leurbost and Laxay.

Wool for Ewe: 36 Kenneth St, Stornoway, HS1 2DR. Tel: 01851 700959.

Stornoway also boasts 'An Lanntair,' an arts centre near the town centre. This vibrant hub includes a cinema, art gallery, café, and restaurant and is open throughout the week from 10 am to 5 pm.

For those interested in Harris Tweed, a more extensive selection can be found in Tarbert, near the ferry terminal and the Harris Distillery. This shop features various Harris Tweed items, from clothes and bags to jackets and trinkets, suitable for all budgets. It's well worth a visit as you pass by, as something special might catch your eye.

Every village across the island likely has a local artisan crafting unique items and selling them directly from their property. As you journey through these villages, watch for signs that might say "Jumpers," "Tweed for Sale," or something similar. These signs are your gateway to discovering a world of handcrafted treasures, from teddy bears, hats, scarves, and gloves to book covers and pictures. The variety of items you can find is virtually endless; each imbued with the personal touch and skill of the maker.

Harris Tweed

Harris Tweed, emblematic of Scottish heritage and craftsmanship, is a distinguished fabric originating from the Outer Hebrides, particularly the Isle of Harris. This textile, deeply ingrained in the cultural tapestry of the Western Isles, boasts a rich history and unique attributes.

Centuries ago, Harris Tweed began as a home-based craft in the rural communities of the Outer Hebrides, where islanders hand weave the fabric using locally dyed and spun wool. This practice, mirroring the islanders' rugged landscape and resilient spirit, evolved into a significant livelihood.

Legally protected by the Harris Tweed Act of 1993, genuine Harris Tweed must be handwoven in the islanders' homes using pure virgin wool from the Outer Hebrides. This strict legal definition safeguards its authenticity and cultural significance. Genuine Harris Tweed will carry the 'Orb' symbol somewhere on the fabric.

The creation of Harris Tweed is a detailed process, beginning with wool shearing and encompassing dyeing, spinning, and hand-weaving on treadle looms, notably the Hattersley loom. The first of these looms arrived in the Hebrides in 1919, revolutionising local weaving. This entire cycle, exclusive to the islands, infuses the fabric with tradition.

Known for its durability, warmth, and moisture resistance, Harris Tweed is ideal for the Scottish climate. It's also lauded for its diverse designs, ranging from classic herringbones to modern patterns.

The Harris Tweed industry underpins the local economy, providing jobs and preserving traditional craftsmanship. Its international acclaim has attracted fashion designers and discerning customers worldwide, maintaining a deep connection to its origins despite its global popularity.

On the world's fashion stages, Harris Tweed has been embraced by top designers for its quality and versatility. Showcased in major fashion capitals, it features in everything from avant-garde to chic contemporary attire, including a range of accessories. Its sustainable production process aligns with the increasing demand for ethical fashion, enhancing its appeal.

Innovative uses of Harris Tweed in fashion, through new dyeing methods and weaving patterns, demonstrate its adaptability. Collaborations between designers and Hebridean weavers have led to unique creations, deepening appreciation for the fabric's 'artisanship'.

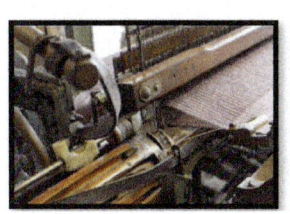

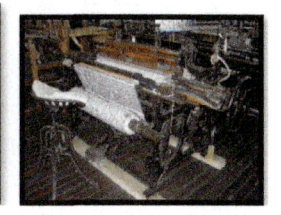

In summary, Harris Tweed bridges the traditional Western Isles weaving with the dynamic realm of high fashion, symbolising a fusion of heritage, craftsmanship, and modern style. More than just a textile, it represents the living heritage and enduring legacy of the Outer Hebrides, a testament to the region's history, culture, and artistry.

Principal Harris Tweed Mills in the Western Isles:
    Kenneth MacKenzie Ltd - Caberfeidh Road, Stornoway, HS1 2SJ.
    Carloway Mill Harris Tweed Ltd - (The oldest Mill with a visitor

centre) -

Carloway, Isle of Lewis, HS2 9AG.

Harris Tweed Hebrides - North Shawbost, Isle of Lewis, HS2 9BD.

10

Hebridean Heritage Sites

Callanish is famous for its Standing Stones.

The site includes a visitor shop, a café area, and ample parking for cars and coaches. It tends to get crowded, especially in the early afternoons during tourist season, and the lower parking area near the main entrance often fills up quickly. Therefore, when I bring guests, I prefer parking at the top area near the Stones, which provides convenient access while avoiding the busy lower lot.

Additionally, close by is the Callanish Alpacas, an engaging attraction where you can learn about these fascinating animals and even have the opportunity to feed them.

CALLANISH ALPACAS

As you follow the road and navigate a few bends, you'll arrive at the village of Dun Carloway, home to 'the Broch.' You'll find parking facilities here, and visiting the best preserved Broch in Scotland atop its rocky knoll is free of charge. Standing about 9 meters tall, this structure is debated to have been constructed around 200 BC. - 1 AD. Historically, it's famed as a stronghold used by the Morrison clan during the 1500s. A Broch is a unique drystone hollow-walled structure from the Iron Age, found exclusively in Scotland.

Gearrannan Blackhouse Village in Garenin in Carloway is a working museum with a rentable hostel that can accommodate medium-sized parties. There is also a visitor shop with a small tea room.

- **Gearrannan Blackhouse Village** - 5A Garenin, Isle of Lewis HS2 9AL. Tel: 01851 643416. It is open Monday - Saturday from 9.30am - 5.30pm.

The Norse Mill at the edge of South Shawbost is a small restored Viking mill you can park and walk to via a small stone-graded path. The walk will take about five to ten minutes as the Mill is not visible from the road.

Gearrannan Blackhouse Village

Norse Mill in South Shawbost

The Whale Bone Arch in Bragar frames a private residence entrance gate, but the public can take pictures at the gate. The bones stand upright, making an arch, and have one of the harpoons used at the time of harvest (which only got 'stuck' in the whale and did not actually detonate until much later once out of the whale) braced between the two bones at the apex of the bones. The bones had been degrading over time and were sent away a few years ago to have fibreglass replicas made. These will last longer in the climate but still look like the real thing.

TRAVEL GUIDE TO LEWIS AND HARRIS

The Blackhouse in Arnol (known as 'Arnol Blackhouse') is a restored and operational blackhouse from the mid-late 1800s, cared for and run by Historic Scotland. Entry fees apply, and be aware that the inside of the blackhouse will be very smokey as the peat is burned in the floor fire (as it was when it was lived in) when it is open to the public. When you enter the door, the people lived on the right-hand side while animals (cow/sheep/goat) are kept on the left so that the sloping ground carries away whatever the animals drop.

- **Arnol Blackhouse** - 42 Arnol, Bragar, Isle of Lewis, HS2 9DB. Tel:

01851 710395. Opening Times From 1 Apr to 30 Sept: Daily except Sun, 9.30 am to 5 pm with last entry at 4 pm. 1 Oct to 31 Mar: Daily except Wednesday and Sunday, 10 am to 4 pm with last entry 3 pm. Price of admission: Adult (16-64 years) -£7.50. Concession (65 years+ and unemployed) - £6.00. Child (7-15 years) - £4.50. Family (1 adult, 2 children)- £15.00. Family (2 adults, 2 children) - £21.50. Family (2 adults, 3 children) - £25.50.

In a little village called Rodel in Harris is St Clement's Church. This little medieval church was founded by the 8th clan chief MacLeod in the 16th century. Today, it is cared for by Historic Scotland. The church holds a few well-preserved Celtic gravestones.

Entrance to the well-cared-for grounds and a small church is free, with a small donation box on the premises.

Hebrides People (formerly Seallam) - Visitor Centre An Taobh Tuath (Northton), Isle of Harris HS3 3JA.

Here, Tracing Genealogy is for anyone wanting to find their roots in the Islands, and they have an unrivalled collection of Island books on sale to the public.

11

Security, Health and Pets

Stornoway's single police station is conveniently located further up Church Street, beyond the Church Street Chippy. While police officers might not be a common sight walking the streets, they do conduct patrols. According to crime statistics.co.uk, the crime rate last month in Stornoway was zero. The island's separation by water from the mainland and the close-knit community contribute to this low crime rate. Here, Neighbors look out for each other, and neighbourhood watch areas take their role seriously, often keeping binoculars handy for monitoring.

- **Stornoway Police Station** - 18 Church Street, Stornoway, Isle of Lewis, HS1 2JD.

There are clinics in most villages along the main roads in Lewis for medical needs, including Leurbost, Carloway, Tolsta, and Habost. The Western Isles Hospital, located on the outskirts of Stornoway on Macaulay Road, offers comprehensive services, including A&E, maternity wards, dental care, a day hospital, and a helipad. The staff are known for their friendliness and kindness. There are also two separate dental practices in Stornoway – Bayhead Dental Practice and Castle View Dental Practice – both equipped to handle emergencies. If you're in pain, dialling 111 connects you to a medical advisor who can assist further.

- **Western Isle Dental Centre** - MacAulay Road, Stornoway, Isle of Lewis, HS1 2BB. Tel: 01851 707500.
- **Castleview Dental Practice** - 79 Cromwell Street, Stornoway, Isle of Lewis, HS1 2DG. Tel: 01851 704400. Email: castleview.dental-practice@nhs.

Pet owners will find excellent care at the Old Mill Veterinary Practice, which is open Monday to Saturday from 9 am to 5:30 pm, with a vet on standby after hours. They offer grooming services and sell a selection of pet accessories. However, be cautious about squeaking toys in the presence of dogs – it can lead to some excitement!

- **Old Mill Vets** - Sandwick Rd, Stornoway HS1 2SL. Tel: 01851 705900. Opening hours are Monday - Friday, 9 am - 5 pm, and Saturdays, 10 am - 4 pm.

For pet supplies, the Tesco and Co-Op stores have a decent range. Additionally, WillowGlen Garden Centre is a dedicated pet shop offering a variety of pet treats, foods, toys, jackets, collars, leads, treats, and even pets like hamsters, bearded dragons, fish, and budgies. The garden centre also sells plants, seeds, garden furniture, bird feeders, large outdoor plant pots, and garden tools. They even house a flower shop with beautiful bouquets and convincingly realistic faux-flowers.

The island's wildlife is diverse, including eagles, dolphins, porpoises, various breeds of sheep, Highland cows, rabbits, deer, and the elusive corncrake.

The Western Isles Hospital, located in Stornoway on the Isle of Lewis, is the main hospital serving the Outer Hebrides in Scotland. Officially opened in 1992, this hospital represents a critical healthcare hub for the region, offering a comprehensive range of services, including accident and emergency, medical and surgical care, maternity services, and various outpatient clinics. It has modern facilities to ensure high-quality patient care, including diagnostic services such as a small laboratory and an x-ray department. The hospital also serves the scattered and remote communities across the Isles, often coordinating with air and ambulance services for emergency transport and patient transfers. As a community-focused institution, Western Isles Hospital is integral not only in providing essential health services but also in supporting the unique needs of the island populations and addressing challenges posed by the remote geography of the Hebrides. The hospital's staff, comprising a mix of local and visiting professionals, are dedicated to offering compassionate care, reflecting the close-knit community spirit of the Isles.

- **Western Isles Hospital** - Macaulay Rd, Stornoway HS1 2AF.

12

Leisure and Recreation

On days when the weather is inclement but you're still keen to engage in some sporting activities, the Sports Centre in Stornoway is the perfect destination. This facility boasts a large swimming pool, complete with a smaller adjacent pool for babies. At certain times, the staff bring out a giant air slide and various pool toys for the children to enjoy under the watchful eyes of the lifeguards.

Adjacent to the pool area, a relaxing space includes a sauna, steam room, shower, and a bubble pool. Conveniently, this area has a 'through the window,' allowing you to keep an eye on your older children enjoying themselves in the main pool while you relax in the bubble pool.

The centre also features indoor courts for sports like squash and badminton, indoor and outdoor facilities for 5-a-side football, an internal climbing wall, a small café, and a well-equipped gym. You can purchase various water-related items at the reception, such as swimsuits, armbands, nose grips, and goggles and there is a small cafe where you can sit and watch the pool activity through the glass windows.

For changing and freshening up, there's a universal changing area with individual rooms, lockers, and several larger changing rooms suitable for families. Additionally, hair dryers are available which, as some of the younger visitors have discovered, can be used creatively to invent new hairstyles.

- **Lewis Sports Centre** - 2 Springfield Rd, Stornoway HS1 2PZ. Tel: 01851 822800.

Leisure Sports

For those who love golf, there are two golf courses. One is in Stornoway, the other in Harris.

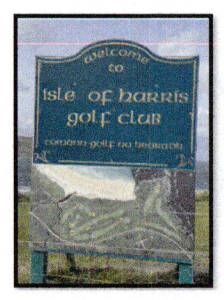

Stornoway has a course of 18 holes set amidst the trees on the castle grounds. Harris has a course of 9 holes, which Nick Faldo and Ronan Rafferty have played! Many people come to play, and many celebrate their small wins.

Shinty and Football are well-developed sports on the Island, and if you come during the league season, you should be able to attend a game for free.

Comann Camanachd Leòdhais, the senior shinty team hailing from the Isle of Lewis, made a historic entry into the league system in 2011. This marked the first time a team from the Western Isles was permitted to compete in league shinty. This was a significant milestone considering the team's introduction was initially on a trial basis to assess the feasibility of long-term participation for the island club.

Although the club finished at the bottom of the league in their debut season, they completed all their fixtures and earned three points. This performance was commendable, especially compared to other teams' debut seasons. Their commitment to fair play was recognised in October 2011 when they received the Marine Harvest (now known as MOWI) National Fairplay Award.

The successful completion of their first season led to Lewis being granted permanent membership in the league, a testament to their perseverance and dedication. Since then, the club has consistently fulfilled every fixture, showcasing the team's strong character and commitment to the sport.

The Lewis and Harris Football Association represents football in the Western Isles. With most areas of the Island having their team (Back, Lochs, Harris, Westside, Point... and more) and supporters, keeping track of all the matches, times, and scores can get a bit confusing. To keep everything clear, the LHFA have their website where everything is clear, concise and it's easy to follow your favourite team - https://www.lhfa.org.uk

Shinty can look violent, and it is! Our daughter can be seen above going for a hit with her Caman, which no one could touch when she had it at home. The ball used in the game is rather sturdy and can leave a nice bruise when it impacts the body. These players are braver than you think, as they do not wear any protection other than shin guards and helmets!

For The Adults

There is the Hebridean Spa on Tong Road in Stornoway for those needing some pampering, relaxation or rejuvenation. They have a hot tub, a massage room and a licensed bar! Booking here could be a whole day experience - it is your holiday. Have a sauna, relax in the lounge, and dip into the hot tub before a full body massage (or specialist massage treatments) - all while trying to hold onto and drink the beverage you choose from the gazebo bar.

- **Hebridean Spa** - 26 Tong Road, Stornoway, Isle of Lewis HS2 0JF. Tel: 07939991578. Opening hours: Monday - Saturday: 10 am - 4 pm, 6 pm - 10 pm. Closed on Sunday. Hebspa.co.uk

Things to do with the Kids

When the rain starts and you're with kids, unsure of what to do, a great indoor option is Adventure Island, located behind Tesco. This 'soft play' area is perfect for children from babies up to ten years old. It operates on a 'pay-to-enter' system. Inside, the children can take off their shoes and explore a climbing unit with three levels, complete with various routes, two slides, and a ball pool. There's also a dedicated, safer area with 'soft blocks' for those under three. The kitchen is ready to take your orders, offering a kid-friendly menu. The reception area doubles as a coffee spot for adults, and a tempting array of desserts displayed in a glass cabinet will catch the younger ones' attention.

On sunny days, there's no shortage of outdoor activities for children. A great starting point is the Castle grounds, which offer several walking paths through trees that Sir James and Lady Matheson planted in the 19th century. Additionally, an 'explore' trail featuring wooden carvings of creatures from the 'Gruffalo' storybook has been added, posing a fun challenge to find all the figures.

LEISURE AND RECREATION

If you're willing to venture further, Ness provides a playpark by the sea, complemented by quaint tea rooms and beaches to explore. Ness also houses a 10-pin bowling alley, a hit with all ages, but remember to book in advance, particularly for weekend slots in the summer. Along the road to Harris, you'll find a large woodland walk with a play park, ideal for enjoying nature and having a picnic. Shawbost and Tarbert (Harris) schools also have swimming pools open to the public, providing another enjoyable activity.

Aline Community Woodland Walk

Situated roughly 20 miles from both Stornoway on Lewis and Tarbert on Harris, Aline Community Woodland can be found along the A859. This welcoming outdoor space features accessible boardwalks and tracks, perfect for leisurely strolls. Visitors can enjoy picnic areas with table benches and a playground for children. Convenient parking is available for cars, coaches/camper vans and is complete with litter and dog waste disposal bins. It is a place that families love to return to again and again.

Starting from the car park, a well-maintained track winds its way down to the shores of Loch Seaforth, located just a mile away. Loch Seaforth, notable for being the longest fjord-like sea loch in the archipelago, is an excellent spot for observing white-tailed eagles. This location is significant as it was here that white-tailed eagles first successfully bred in Lewis following their reintroduction. The area continues to be a popular habitat for both white-tailed and golden eagles. While golden eagles are often spotted soaring over distant ridges, the surrounding woodland is also home to a pair of sparrow hawks. These eagle species, buzzards and sparrow hawks are visible throughout the year.

White-tailed eagles are distinguishable from golden eagles in flight by their broader wings and shorter, wedge-shaped tails. They also have a more pronounced head and bill. Often referred to as "sea eagles" due to their size, these majestic birds offer a unique wildlife-watching experience in the region.

SeaTrek -

For over 40 years, SeaTrek has been offering unforgettable maritime adventures around Uig, utilising sturdy, rigid, inflatable boats to navigate the stunning Atlantic sea stacks.

Fishing enthusiasts, whether beginners or seasoned anglers, can immerse themselves in a fulfilling Sea Fishing Trip in Uig. SeaTrek provides all necessary fishing equipment and waterproof gear, ensuring a comfortable and enjoyable experience. The waters around Uig teem are full of diverse fish species and offer an exciting fishing experience.

Anglers might encounter a variety of fish in these fertile waters. The tide races around rocky headlands that are abundant with Pollock and saithe, while varied seabed conditions yield haddock and whiting. The underwater reefs are hotspots for catching cod and ling. Thornbacks and flatfish are commonly found in the shallower inshore areas of mud and sand.

Another highlight is the Sea Eagles and Lagoon trip, departing from Miavaig's jetty in Uig. This journey takes you through Loch Roag, past Reef, and into Little Loch Roag, a prime spot for spotting otters along the shoreline. Sea Eagles, also known as White Tailed Sea Eagles, frequently showcase their majesty over these waters. The trip continues to Traigh na Berie, Siaram, and Pabbay Mor, where you can marvel at the stunning sea caves, natural arches, and a spectacular Lagoon. The trip includes a chance to interact with local marine life, like seals, and the excitement of lobster potlifting.

The 2-hour RIB trip to Gallan Head is perfect for those seeking awe-inspiring landscapes. This journey offers breathtaking views of Reef Beach, Pabbay, and Cliff Bay and passes through impressive sea caves. Gallan Head, the most northwesterly point of the UK, is a haven for diverse marine wildlife. The trip might also include a visit to Harsgeir and Vacasay, both rich in birdlife and home to seals, and an opportunity to check lobster pots.

Lastly, the Island Trip is a blend of wildlife viewing and exploration. After cruising and observing local wildlife, you'll land on one of Loch Roag's scenic islands, such as Little Bernera or Pabbay. These islands, steeped in history and natural beauty, offer perfect spots for picnicking or hiking. However, due to the nature of the landing, this trip is not recommended for those with restricted mobility. Little Bernera, a historically significant island, showcases remnants of its past, including ancient gravestones and a ruined chapel.

- **SeaTrek** - Miavaig, Isle of Lewis, HS2 9HE. Tel: 01851 672469.

Each SeaTrek journey promises a unique and enriching experience tailored to all ages and interests, making every trip a memorable part of your visit to Uig with all the above and more.

Surfing

Surfing in the Western Isles of Scotland, particularly on the Isle of Lewis and Harris, offers some of Europe's most spectacular and challenging surfing opportunities. These islands are known for their pristine, unspoiled beaches and powerful Atlantic swells, making them a coveted destination for surfers. The best time for surfing in this region typically falls between late autumn and early spring, when the North Atlantic swell is at its peak.

Notable Surf Spots:

Dalmore Beach: Located on the Isle of Lewis, Dalmore Beach is known for its consistent waves and beautiful scenery. It's suitable for both beginners and experienced surfers.

Scarista Beach: On the Isle of Harris, Scarista Beach is revered for its stunning setting and offers excellent wave conditions, particularly for more experienced surfers.

Weather and Water Conditions:

- The water temperatures in the Western Isles are generally cold,

requiring a good-quality wetsuit, boots, gloves, and a hood.
- The weather can be quite changeable, so surfers should be prepared for varying conditions.

Surf Schools and Equipment Hire:

- There are surf schools available that offer lessons and equipment hire. These schools cater to all experience levels and are an excellent option for those new to surfing or looking to improve their skills.

Safety and Local Advice:

- Given the remote nature of many surf spots, it's essential to be mindful of safety. Surfing with a buddy, being aware of the tides and local weather conditions, and respecting local guidelines and advice are crucial.
- Local surf shops and schools are excellent resources for up-to-date information on surfing conditions and safety advice.

Wildlife and Environment:

- The Western Isles are home to diverse wildlife, and it's not uncommon for surfers to encounter marine animals such as seals or dolphins. Respect for the natural environment and wildlife is paramount.

Community and Culture:

- Though relatively small, the surfing community in the Western Isles is welcoming and passionate about their sport. Surfing here also offers a chance to immerse oneself in the unique culture and heritage of the islands.

Overall, surfing in the Western Isles is about more than just the sport; it's an experience that encompasses the awe-inspiring natural beauty, unique culture, and the thrilling challenge of surfing in the cold, wild waters of the Atlantic.

- **SurfLewis** - Tel: 07920 427 194.

13

Other Helpful Places

For those needing banking services during their stay, Stornoway offers four banks and a main Post Office to cater to your financial needs. The banks available are:

- **The Bank of Scotland** - 47 Cromwell St, Stornoway HS1 2DD. Open from 9.30am - 3.30pm Monday to Friday.
- **The Royal Bank of Scotland** - 47 Cromwell St, Stornoway HS1 2DD. Open from 9.30am - 3.30pm Monday to Friday.
- **Virgin Money** - 23 South Beach, 2BQ, Stornoway HS1 2BQ. 9.30am - 4pm Monday, Tuesday, Thursday and Friday. Wednesday is 10am - 4pm.
- **TSB** - 18 Francis St, Stornoway HS1 2NB. This bank holds hours similar to the Virgin Money bank, but it also closes for lunch between 1.30pm - 2.30pm each day.
- **Post Office** - 16 Francis Street in Stornoway. Open from 9.30am - 5.30pm Monday to Friday. Open on Saturdays from 9am until 12.30pm

The Post Office and the TSB bank are on a side street away from the town center, but all the other banks can be found along the main street as you journey through town.

If you need more straightforward DIY repair items, Tesco stocks a range of essentials like glues, small sewing packs, needles, scissors, and threads in various colors. For a more extensive selection of threads, needles, and other craft or DIY items, the Hobby Shop at the end of Cromwell Street is your go-to destination as you leave the town center.

- **The Hebridean Hobby Centre** - 97 Cromwell St, Stornoway HS1 2DG. Tel: 01851 703366.

Other noteworthy DIY and home improvement shops include:

- **Aladdin's Cave** - 2 Inaclete Rd, Stornoway HS1 2RB. Tel: 01851 703253.
- **Crofters** - Island Rd, Stornoway HS1 2RD. Tel: 01851 702350.
- **Home Improvement Centre** (which has an impressive kitchen section featuring travel mugs and similar items) - 20 Bells Rd, Stornoway HS1 2RA. Tel: 01851 703646.
- **MacGregor Industrial Supplies** - 20 Bells Rd, Stornoway HS1 2RA. Tel: 01851 706799.

MacGregor specialises in hardware like screws, screwdrivers, tools, chains of various sizes, toolboxes, and other items that might be tempting for those with a penchant for handiwork.

Tourist Information

For tourist information, the town centre houses a well-stocked and helpful Tourist Information shop known as Visit Stornoway iCentre. Parking is available behind the shop in what residents call the 'small car park,' which operates on a pay and display system, except for those with a valid disabled card.

- **Visit Stornoway iCentre** - 26 Cromwell St, Stornoway HS1 2DD. Tel: 01851 703088.

Church Denominations

If you are staying through a weekend and want to go to a church, there are a few denominations to choose from:

OTHER HELPFUL PLACES

- **Associated Presbyterian Churches**: Stornoway and Harris (APC) - 72 Keith St, Stornoway, Isle of Lewis HS1 2JG.
- **The Church of Scotland:** Martin's Memorial Church - 11 Francis Street, Stornoway Isle of Lewis, HS1 2NB; - Stornoway High Church - Matheson Rd, Stornoway HS1 2NQ; - St Columba's (Old Parish) Church - Lewis St, Stornoway HS1 2JF.
- **The Free Church of Scotland:** Kenneth St, Stornoway, HS1 2DR.
- **The Free Church of Scotland** (Continuing): Sandwick Rd, Stornoway HS1 2HE.
- **The Free Presbyterian Church of Scotland:** Scotland St, Stornoway, HS1 2JR.
- **The Reform Presbyterian Church of Scotland:** Bridge Community Centre, Bayhead Embankment, Stornoway HS1 2EB.
- **The Roman Catholic Church:** 71 Kenneth St, Stornoway HS1 2DS.
- **The Salvation Army** - Bayhead, Stornoway HS1 2DZ.
- **The Scottish Episcopal Church:** Francis St, Stornoway HS1 2ND.
- **The Stornoway Baptist Church** - 60 Seaforth Rd, Stornoway HS1 2SH.
- **The New Wine Church:** Barvas & Brue Community Centre - Barvas, Isle of Lewis HS2 0RA.

Most church services start at 11 am and last for about 60 - 90 minutes.

It is helpful to remember that most of the food shops are closed on Sundays.

14

Notable Beaches of the Island

So you want to go to a beach?

The Outer Hebrides are renowned for their stunning landscapes, which include pristine sandy beaches, rolling moorlands, and rugged mountains. The beaches are particularly famous for their white sands and turquoise waters, resembling more tropical destinations. The beaches in the Outer Hebrides are perhaps the most visually striking feature. Places like Luskentyre, Seilebost, and Scarista on the Isle of Harris have vast expanses of white sandy beaches that contrast sharply with the clear blue waters of the Atlantic. These beaches are often secluded and offer a sense of peace and natural beauty that is hard to find elsewhere.

A few beaches of note:

- **Luskentyre Beach (Isle of Harris):** It is known for its vast expanses of white sand and turquoise waters; it's often rated as one of the best beaches in the UK.
- **Seilebost Beach (Isle of Harris):** A beautiful, less crowded beach with spectacular views, particularly of the North Harris hills.
- **Scarista Beach (Isle of Harris):** Offers a stunning combination of golden sand and rugged terrain, popular among surfers and walkers.
- **Traigh Mhor (Isle of Barra):** Famous for being a beach runway for small aircraft, it's a unique spot with beautiful views.
- **Uig Sands (Isle of Lewis):** A vast area of sand and dunes offers incredible scenery and a sense of isolation.
- **Clachan Sands (North Uist):** Known for its white sands and clear waters, providing a tranquil and picturesque setting.
- **Berneray West Beach (Berneray):** Offers miles of unspoiled sandy beach with views of Harris and the surrounding islands.
- **Hosta Beach (North Uist):** A beautiful and remote beach known for its big waves and popular among surfers.

- **Tolsta Beach (Isle of Lewis):** A stunning long sandy beach surrounded by cliffs and moorland.
- **Vatersay Beach (Isle of Vatersay):** A beautiful, secluded beach with fine white sand, crystal-clear waters, and a serene atmosphere.
- **Bosta Beach (Great Bernera, Lewis):** A lovely, remote beach with historical significance, known for its Iron Age house reconstruction.
- **Tangasdale Beach (Isle of Barra):** Offers dramatic views, especially at sunset, with golden sands and rugged hills in the background.
- **Dalmore Beach (Isle of Lewis):** Known for its dramatic waves and strong currents, making it popular among surfers.
- **Shawbost Beach (Isle of Lewis):** A picturesque beach with a combination of sand and rocky outcrops, rich in wildlife and historical interest.

Each beach has unique charm and beauty, making the Western Isles a remarkable destination for beach lovers and nature enthusiasts.

NOTABLE BEACHES OF THE ISLAND

15

Maps

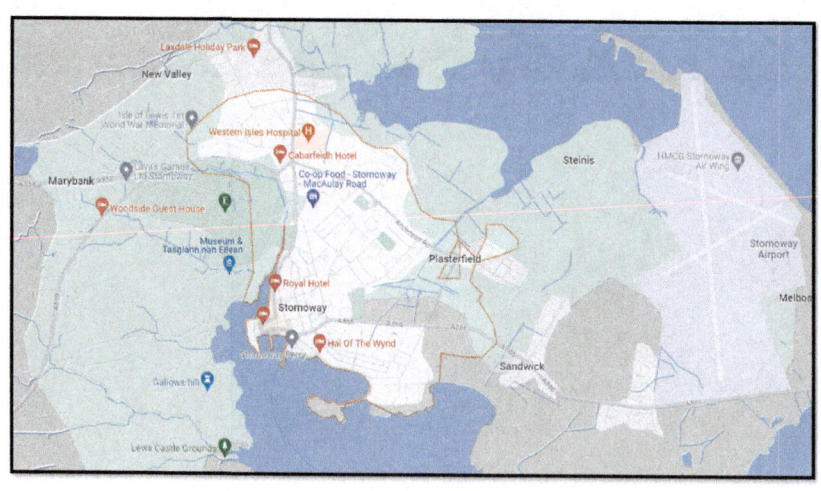

GoogleMaps – Stornoway

MAPS

Google Maps – Gearrannan Blackhouse village

Google Maps – Callanish Stones and Stone Circles

TRAVEL GUIDE TO LEWIS AND HARRIS

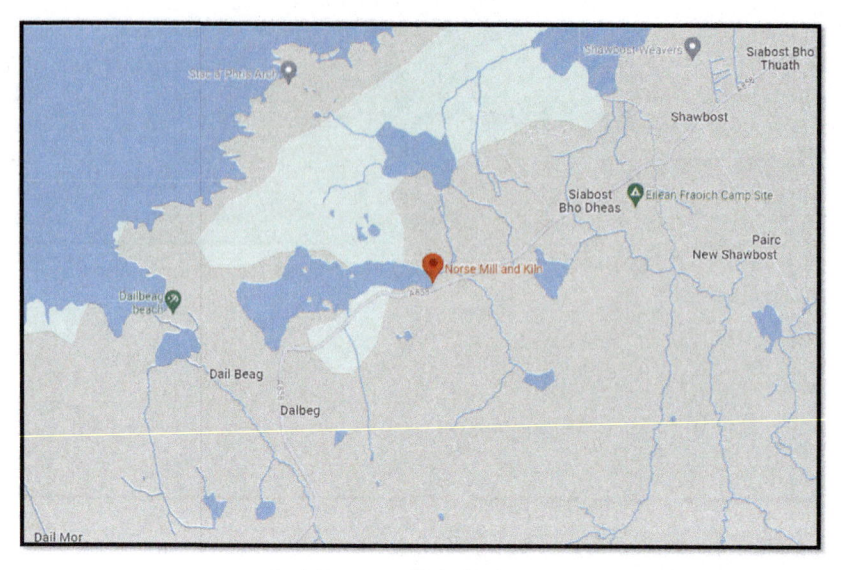

Google Maps – Norse Mill, Isle of Lewis.

Google Maps – Whalebone Arch, Bragar, Isle of Lewis.

MAPS

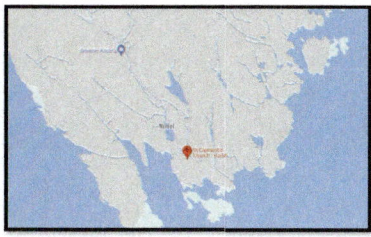

Google Maps – St Clement's Church, Rodel, Isle of Harris

Google Maps Churches in Stornoway

Google Maps - Charity Shops in Stornoway

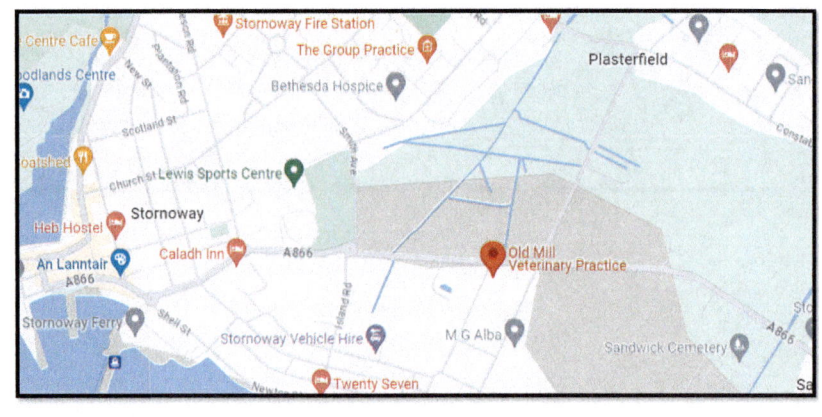

Google Maps – Old Mill Vets, Stornoway

MAPS

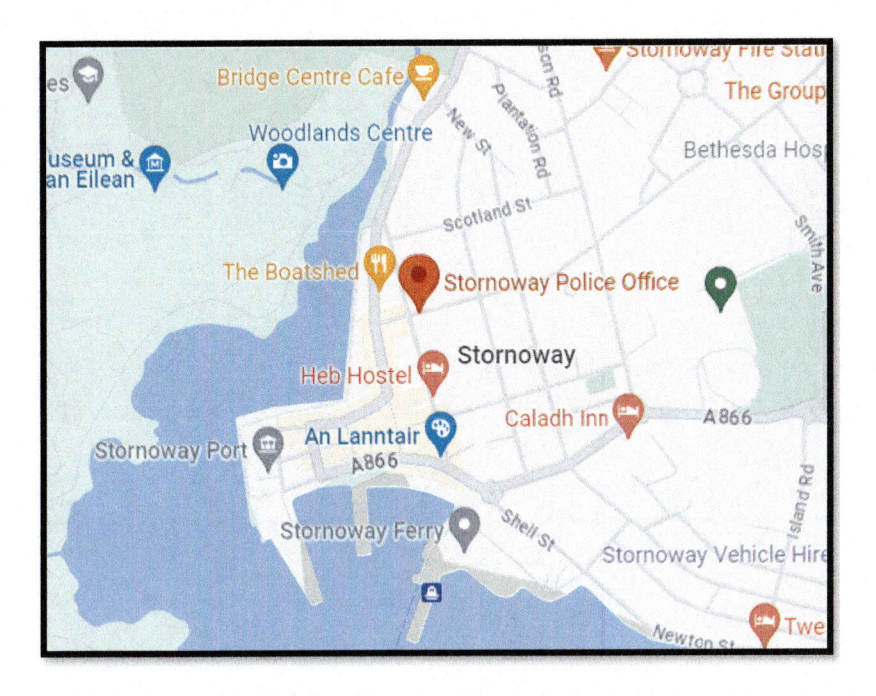

Google Maps – Police Station, Church St, Stornoway

Google Maps – Taxi Ranks in Stornoway

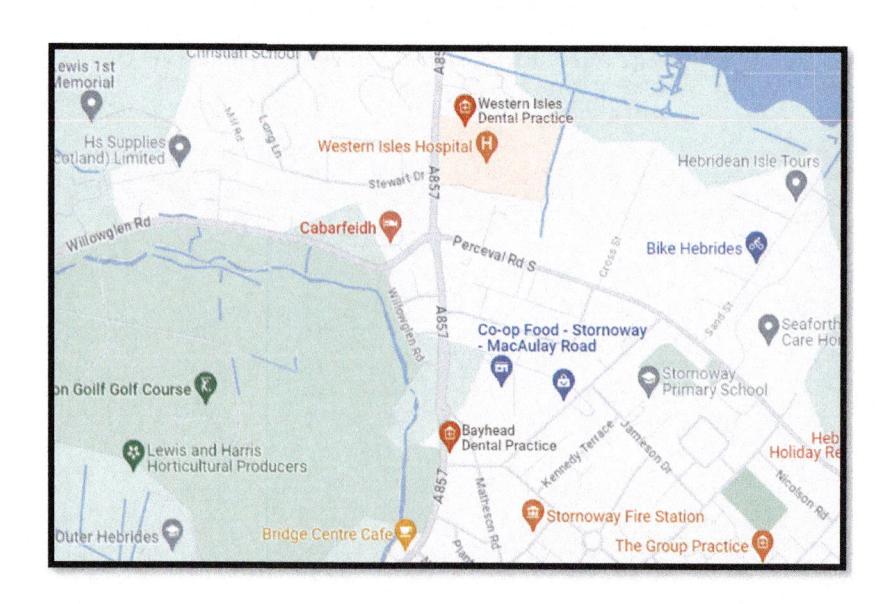

Google Maps – Dental Clinics in Stornoway

MAPS

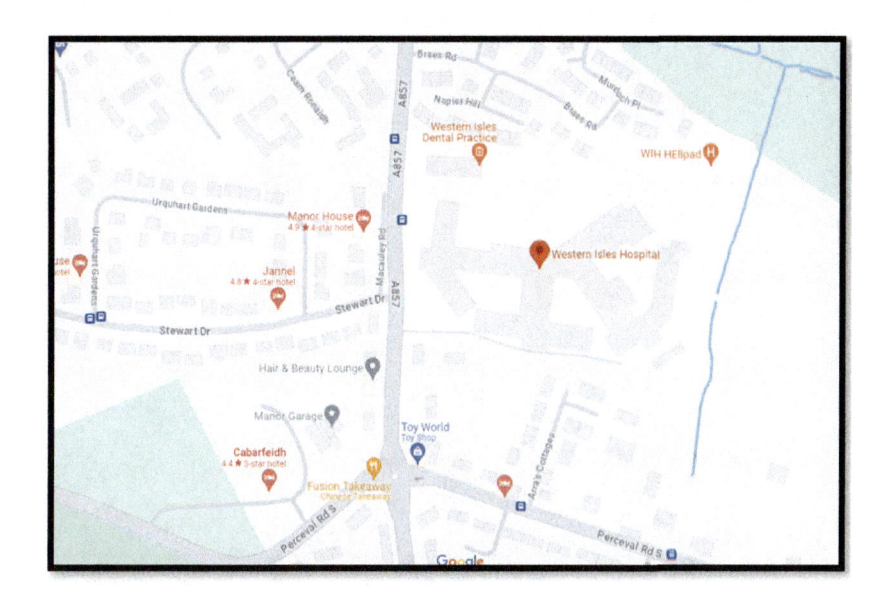

Google Maps - Western Isles Hospital

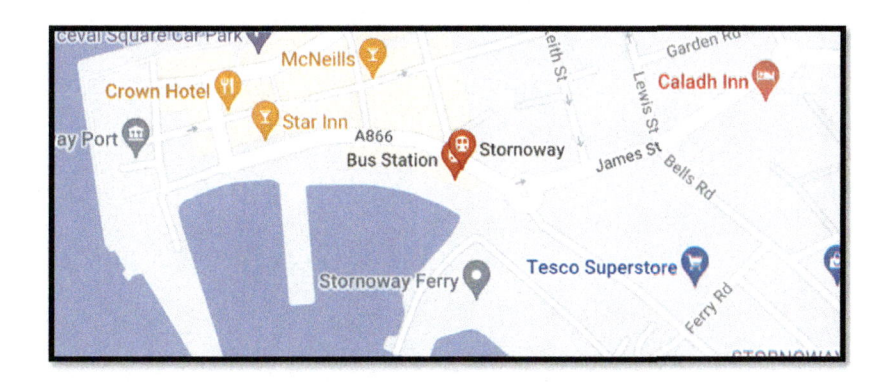

Google Maps – Stornoway Bus Station

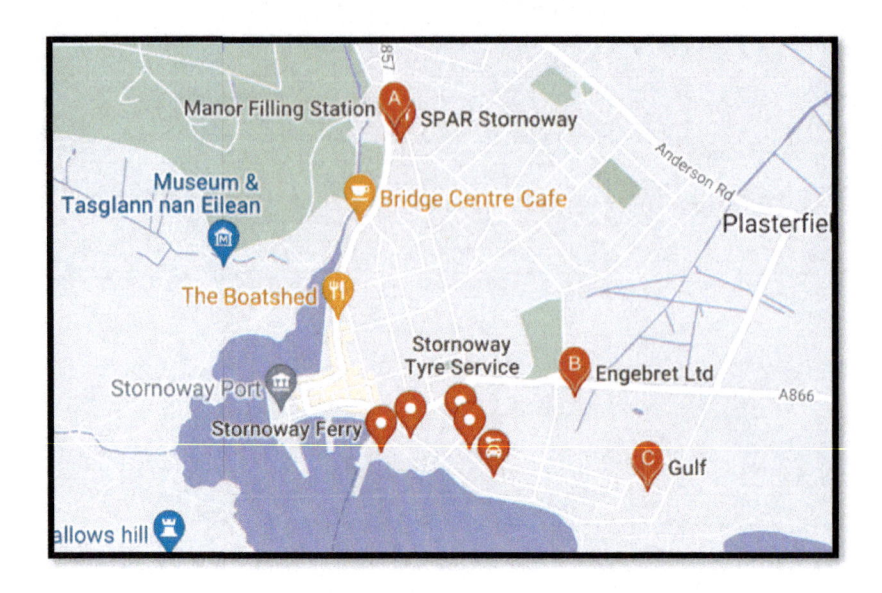

Google Maps - Petrol / Gas Stations in Stornoway

16

In Conclusion

In conclusion, the Western Isles of Scotland, a chain of islands on the edge of the Atlantic, are a testament to nature's enduring beauty and resilience. From the pristine white sands of Luskentyre Beach to the ancient, mysterious Callanish Standing Stones, these islands weave a tapestry of breathtaking landscapes and profound cultural heritage. Each island's unique character tells a story of a land shaped by the elements and enriched by a strong community spirit.

Watercolours by artist Alan Wilson – 2021

The Outer Hebrides is a destination and a journey into a world where nature's drama unfolds at every turn. The rugged mountains of Harris, the vast peat moors of Lewis, and the vibrant machair with its seasonal blooms offer more than just scenic beauty; they invite a deeper connection with the natural world. The islands' rich Gaelic heritage, reflected in music, language, and folklore, adds another layer to their allure, which makes visiting here a truly immersive experience.

Whether it's walking along the tranquil beaches of Barra, exploring the historical ruins on the Isle of Berneray, or experiencing the unique wildlife and birdlife that call these islands home, the Western Isles promises memories that last a lifetime. They challenge us to rethink our relationship with the environment and offer a refuge for those seeking solace in the lap of unspoiled nature.

As this booklet closes, it leaves an open invitation to explore the Western Isles, embrace their untamed beauty, and discover the rhythms of island life. Here, against the backdrop of the Atlantic, you'll find a place where time slows down and the simple joys of nature's grandeur take centre stage. The Western Isles are not just a place to visit; they are a world to experience, cherish, and remember.

IN CONCLUSION

Tapadh Leat (Thank you)

17

Resources

Welcome to the Outer Hebrides. (n.d.). Outer Hebrides. https://www.visitouterhebrides.co.uk

Car & Van Rental | Car Hire Hebrides. (n.d.). Car Hire Hebrides. https://www.carhire-hebrides.co.uk

Encyclopedia Britannica. (n.d.). Encyclopedia Britannica. https://www.britannica.com

Isle of Harris Distillery | Isle of Harris Distillery. (n.d.). Isle of Harris Distillery. https://www.harrisdistillery.com

Hebridean Spa. (n.d.). https://hebspa.co.uk

Kristin. (2023, October 8). Scotland Less Explored - Travel advice for off the beaten path Scotland. *Scotland Less Explored*. https://www.scotlandlessexplored.com

RESOURCES

Isle of Harris Golf Course. (n.d.). https://www.harrisgolf.com

Historic Environment Scotland. (2023, October 25). Àrainneachd Eachdraidheil Alba. https://www.historicenvironment.scot/

Old Mill Veterinary Practice. (n.d.). https://www.oldmillvets.co.uk

Abhainn Dearg Distillery | Isle of Lewis. (n.d.). https://abhainndeargdistillery.co.uk

Curious and wondrous travel destinations - Atlas Obscura. (n.d.). Atlas Obscura.
  https://www.atlasobscura.com

Historic Environment Scotland. (2023, October 25). Àrainneachd Eachdraidheil Alba. https://www.historicenvironment.scot

Whalebone Arch, Bragar, -
   Whalebone Arch Photograph - Abhijit Das - 2021.
   Whalebone Arch Sign Photograph - Abhijit Das - 2021.
   Whalebone Harpoon Photograph - Dan Bacon - 2022.

Alpacas, C. (2020). *Facebook.* [online] www.facebook.com. Available at: https://www.facebook.com/CallanishAlpacas [Accessed 22 Dec. 2023].

Authority, S.P. (2021). *Leisure.* [online] www.stornowayportauthority.com. Available at: https://www.stornowayportauthority.com/sectors/leisure [Accessed 22 Dec. 2023].

Google Maps (2019). *Google Maps.* [online] Google Maps. Available at:

http://www.googlemaps.com.

Printagonist (n.d.). *Map of Harris and Lewis, Outer Hebrides Old Antique Map of Isle of Harris Old Map Wall Print Poster Wall Artwall Art Scottish Maps - Etsy UK*. [online] www.etsy.com. Available at: https://www.etsy.com/uk/Printagonist/listing/1088657914/map-of-harris-and-lewis-outer-hebrides [Accessed 23 Dec. 2023].

Wilson, A. (2019). *Instagram*. [online] www.instagram.com. Available at: https://www.instagram.com/alanwilson376/ [Accessed 23 Dec. 2023].

An Lanntair (n.d.). *An Lanntair*. [online] An Lanntair. Available at: https://lanntair.com [Accessed 23 Dec. 2023].

artuk.org. (n.d.). *Western Isles Hospital | Art UK*. [online] Available at: https://artuk.org/visit/venues/western-isles-hospital-6638 [Accessed 23 Dec. 2023].